The Changed Ones

THE CHANGED ONES;

OR,

REFLECTIONS ON THE SECOND CHAPTER OF THE SONG OF SOLOMON.

BY

REV. FREDERICK WHITFIELD, A.B.,

Late Incumbent of Kirkby-Ravensworth, near Richmond, Yorkshire.

AUTHOR OF "VOICES FROM THE VALLEY," "TRUTH IN CHRIST,"
"SACRED POEMS AND PROSE," ETC., ETC.

LONDON:
S. W. PARTRIDGE 9, PATERNOSTER ROW.

Butler & Tanner,
The Selwood Printing Works,
Frome, and London.

INDEX.

	PAGE
THE CHANGED ONES	1
THE FULNESS OF JESUS	12
THE DISEASE AND ITS REMEDY	20
OUR PLACE AND ITS BLESSINGS	32
THE CHURCH BEHOLDING CHRIST	46
THE EXHORTATION AND MOTIVE	54
THE HIDING PLACE: ITS BLESSINGS AND DANGERS	67
ASSURANCE AND PRAYER	81

PREFACE.

THE following chapters are the substance of an address. It was afterwards suggested to me to issue them in the present form. In compliance with that suggestion, I now send them forth to the public.

The portion of God's holy word on which they treat, is one of the most spiritual and instructive in the book of which it forms a part. I have already considered the first chapter of The Song of Solomon, in my larger work, "Truth in Christ;" and at some future time, if the Lord will, I may probably send forth some thoughts on the remaining chapters of this precious book.

The meaning of the word "lily" is "a changed one." The chapter is simply a narrative of what passes between these changed ones—between the Lord Jesus and His people.

Reader, may your heart and mine deeply experience the truths it brings before our view! May we be one of these changed ones, whose hearts are taken up with Jesus! To live outside of the precious experiences of this chapter, while yet calling ourselves children of God, is a sad state to be in; and yet it is to be feared a state only too prevalent. It may be the state of a Christian, but of a Christian on the low level of the world. No wonder that such a state presents little or no testimony for God before men. No wonder that the life of God in such a soul is in a sickly state, like that of the salt which has lost its savour. If we would know what peace, joy, and superiority to the ever-fretting circumstances of each hour are, we must watch and pray, we must live near to Jesus, lean on His bosom, dwell in His love. Without this the secret heart will soon feel the chilling winds of the world, nipping every bud and blossom and fruit of the Spirit within us.

To know *what* Christianity is, reader, you must *be* a Christian. No one will ever know it without. To know who and what Jesus is, you must live *to* Him, *in* Him, *for* Him. Without this He will scarcely be more to you than a name deeply reverenced.

The day is breaking. The shadows are even now ready to flee away. Oh, to live to Him for the few short days that are still left to us! Let us wake from slumber. Let us wait and work and watch for our precious Lord; and may He find us so doing when He sends for us!

SOUTHGATE, LONDON, N.,
April, 1866.

CHAPTER I.

The Changed Ones.

"I am the rose of Sharon, and the lily of the valleys. As the lily among thorns, so is my love among the daughters. As the apple-tree among the trees of the wood, so is my Beloved among the sons." *Song of Sol.* ii. 1–3.

GOD'S desire is to set Christ before us in all things, so to present Him to our view that we may be won to Him. The heart of man needs only this to make him like God here and to see God hereafter. There is concentrated in Jesus every excellence, every beauty, everything that man needs; and when seen, there is nothing beyond that he desires to see. Heaven is already begun to the soul that sees Jesus. He has learned to sing the new song, he has caught the rapturous echo of the redeemed, his heart has wakened up to the medody of their golden harps. Heaven is in his heart, for he has seen Jesus. And he, alone, who has something of heaven in his heart here, will enter heaven hereafter.

It is thus, this beautiful chapter commences. Jesus is set before us in its very first words—Jesus in all His grace and beauty. He is first named here, because He is first in God's heart. And as Christ is first here, so should He be with us in all things. Everything and every one else secondary.

Reader, bear this in mind. God places Him first here that you should make Him first in everything. Whatever else you forget, never forget this. You may have everything else, everything heaven can bestow and earth can lavish, but if you are without Him, you are but " sounding brass and a tinkling cymbal." You may have earth's beauty, but you are deformity in the sight of heaven. The world may know you for many great and good things, but heaven knows you not. " I never knew you," is God's verdict on all.

"I am the rose of Sharon, and the lily of the valleys." The "rose of Sharon," or flower of the plain, as it is called. The meaning of its name is to love the shade. It is unseen, but sends forth its fragrance. What a beautiful description of the Lord Jesus! To love the shade was the conspicuous feature in His character. Humility shone in meridian rays, in every thought and word and deed. The son of a carpenter, laid in a manger, having not where to lay His head, crucified between two thieves, coming not to do His own will but the will of Him that sent Him,—humility was the culminating feature in His character. "He made Himself of no reputation." "He emptied Himself, and took upon Him the form of a servant." "He humbled Himself, and became obedient unto death, even the death of the cross." My soul, what an example for thee! Art thou proud? Oh what a contradiction to thy Lord and Master! Neither heaven nor earth can furnish a greater. Art thou complacent? Oh, turn and look here, and lie low in the dust! Think of Him, who, though He was humility itself, yet "humbled himself." Art thou making much of thy rank and station, or of thy pedigree and position in life? Think of Him who "emptied himself," nay more, "made himself of no reputation." Oh stoop; lie low at His feet! Be humble, if thou wouldst be like Him. If He, the Lord of glory, humbled Himself, thou, a poor worm of the dust, mayest well do so; thy birthright a sinful body, thy heritage a shroud, a corpse, a grave, and the worms of the dust!

But from this unseen place the rose sends forth its fragrance. What a heavenly halo surrounded that humble Man! What sweetness encircled His dear Name! What a holy fragrance distilled from all His life, from every action and every word! It was the perfume of heaven scattering its healing fragrance over the noxious atmosphere of our fallen world. How did the helpless and needy ones cluster around His path to be blessed! How they hung on the life-giving words that fell from His lips! "What manner of man is this!" were the utterances of those who thronged His path. "Never man spake like this man," was the testimony to His grace and love and power. " Lord, to whom shall we go?" was the deep breathing of many a heart in Galilee. "Surely this was the Son of God," was the testimony of those who had watched Him, and who now stood gazing upon His gaping wounds, as He hung upon the cross. Surely the rose of Sharon was our precious Jesus, loving the shade, and yet from that shade sending forth holy, heavenly fragrance!

And it is ever so that fragrance is the offspring of humility. Do we love the shade? Then we shall speak for Christ; for from humility goeth forth a fragrance which will ever speak for Jesus. We have been in the same school. We have been taught by His Spirit. We have caught a glimpse of Him as He was, and it has left its mark upon us, the mark of heaven.

But He is also "the lily of the valleys." The lily means life—life from the dead. It appears in spring time, and is thus an emblem of resurrection. It is derived from the verb *shanah*, to change, and literally means "a changed one." The Lord Jesus is thus a changed one. No longer the "Man of sorrows, and acquainted with grief," but now in glory. He is the resurrection One—" I am the resurrection and the life," "I am He that liveth and was dead." Once He wore the crown of thorns, now He wears the crown of glory. Once He was the despised and rejected one, now angels veil their faces in His presence, and cry—

"Thrice holy to our God most high,
Thrice holy to our King."

He is "the lily of the *valleys*"—the lily not of one valley but of every valley. There are many kinds of lilies scattered throughout the land, each having beauties and graces peculiar to itself. Here, however, is a lily which possesses in itself the beauty and grace of every kind of lily in whatever valley it may be found. He is "the lily of the *valleys*."

And not only is Christ called a lily but His people are called lilies also. "As the lily among thorns, so is my love among the daughters." She is called *by His name*, for He has *espoused* her to Himself. His name and His nature are upon her. He has made her what she is, and it is His beauty that is seen on her. She too, is a resurrection one, for she is "dead and risen with Christ." She is exhorted to "seek the things that are above" because a risen one with Him. She is a changed one as He is. She is changed from a child of wrath to an heir of heaven. She is washed from her sins in His precious blood. Pardoned, forgiven, and "accepted in the Beloved," she is now one with Him, partaker of the Divine nature, and before God as Christ Himself.

But she is a "lily among thorns." Both grow together here. But how different the end! One to adorn the bosom or the table, the other for the fire.

How deeply suggestive are these figures! Yes, the "thorn" suggests only one thought—the fire. Reader, art thou one? Then read in this expressive figure thy end. Oh, how it should make you tremble! The "devouring fire" now ready to be revealed from heaven shall surround thee, unforgiven one. "Men gather them," says our Lord, "and cast them into the fire, and they are burned." "Men *gather* them!" How expressive! "*Gather* them" as a shepherd gathers his sheep from all the hiding-places whither it has wandered, not leaving one behind, not leaving one path untraversed, not one cleft or bush or thicket unsearched—*gathered* thus for the fire. Oh, how solemn! Reader, think of this gathering of the thorns, and remember it is at hand. Thy days are all numbered. "The Lord is at hand." Haste to the refuge from the gathering storm! Haste sinner, haste, and be reconciled to thy God. Come as a needy, helpless sinner to thy gracious and Almighty Saviour. Look to Him dying on the cross. Believe in that finished work for thy soul. Believe that thy sin is forgiven, thy pardon sealed, thy salvation "finished." Believe it *now*. Believe it and rejoice. Believe it and become a lily— a "changed one."

Reader, art thou a lily? Keep thy garments clean. Thou art washed in the blood of the Lamb. Oh, beware of the defilements around thee! "Touch not the unclean thing." "Abstain from all appearance of evil." You are not your own. You cannot dispose of yourself, or of anything belonging to you, as you please. You are the Lord's. Oh, live to Him, for Him, in Him! Keep down every spirit, every temper, every word that would dishonour Him. Banish every thought, every purpose, every plan that would grieve His blessed Spirit. Keep yourself unspotted from the world. Let the mind of Christ be found in you at all times. Cultivate secret, holy fellowship with God. Let no films or shadows draw a veil between your soul and the brightness of His countenance. Haste with them, *the moment they are felt*, to "the blood." Let nothing harbour or fester in the dark. Go in *thought*, and *at once*, to Him, with every stain and every shadow and every film. Wash in the blood, wash in the blood! So shall thy peace be like a river, and thy joy shall be full.

"I was a wandering sheep,
   I did not love the fold;
 I did not love my Shepherd's voice,
   I would not be controlled.
I was a wayward child,
   I did not love my home,
I did not love my Father's voice,
   I loved afar to roam.

The Shepherd sought His sheep,
   The Father sought His child;
They follow'd me o'er vale and hill,
   O'er deserts waste and wild.
They found me nigh to death,
   Famished and faint and lone;
They bound me with the bands of love;
   They saved the wandering one.

They spoke in tender love,
   They raised my drooping head;
They gently closed my bleeding wounds,
   My fainting soul they fed.

THE CHANGED ONES.

They washed my filth away,
  They made me clean and fair;
They brought me to my home in peace—
  The long-sought wanderer.

Jesus, my Shepherd is;
  'Twas He that loved my soul,
'Twas He that washed me in His blood,
  'Twas He that made me whole.
'Twas He that sought the lost,
  That found the wandering sheep;
'Twas He that brought me to the fold—
  'Tis He that still doth keep.

I was a wandering sheep,
  I would not be controlled;
But now I love my Shepherd's voice,
  I love, I love the fold!
I was a wayward child,
  I once preferred to roam;
But now I love my Father's voice—
  I love, I love His home!"

H. BONAR.

CHAPTER II.

The Fulness of Jesus.

"I sat down under His shadow with great delight, and His fruit was sweet to my taste. He brought me to the banqueting house, and His banner over me was love." *Song of Sol.* ii. 3, 4.

TWO things are remarkable in these verses, and, indeed, throughout this precious book,—personal assurance and individual experience. "*My* love," "*my* beloved," "*my* sister," "*my* spouse," "*my* fair one"—such are the expressions of Christ to His people, and their expressions to Him in return. There is nothing said about pardon, reconciliation, or forgiveness of sins. All this is taken for granted. The soul is standing on the firm rock of conscious forgiveness and assured acceptance in the Beloved, and is *rising from* that ground to *Himself.* It is the counterpart of Paul. He knew he was saved. He stood on that ground, and rose from it to more earnest longings after Jesus Himself. He says, "that I may know *Him*." So with the beloved one in this Song. She *knows* she is saved. She rises from the personal assurance of this to earnest breathing after *Himself*. "Let *Him* kiss me;" "tell me, O Thou whom my soul loveth, where Thou feedest." Such is her language now. And so also as to individual *experience*. "*I* sat down under His shadow with great delight, and His fruit was *sweet to my* taste." "He brought *me* to the *banqueting house*, and His banner over *me* was love." All is *experience*; all is *heart*-work. *Head*-knowledge has no place here. It is only the *heart* that can either see or know Jesus. The *head* may know much about *God;* but about *Jesus* it can know nothing. He makes Himself known to the *heart*, and only to the heart. There He *begins*, there He *continues*, there He *ends*. And when Jesus makes Himself known to the heart, and enters in, there is *heaven*.

The world may have its thoughts of Jesus, it may sing sweet songs of its ideal heaven, its jasper walls and genial air—all this is *sentimental* religion. Into the *true* heaven it cannot enter, for heaven has never entered into the heart. Jesus is unknown, therefore all is visionary, shadowy sentimentalism. The heart that has not seen Jesus knows nothing of heaven—*absolutely* nothing. And the heart that has seen Jesus has a secret it *cannot* tell. It is so real, so deep, so precious, so unutterable, so inexhaustible that it is incommunicable. Reader, wouldst thou know it? Thou must taste it for *thyself*. Worlds cannot tell thee what it is, the redeemed cannot, angels cannot, heaven cannot. It is a *secret;* and the soul that would know *that* secret must know Jesus.

Yet the soul can tell *something* about it though imperfectly, though with lisping, stammering tongue. Reader, canst *thou?* Thou mayest not be able to say *much*, canst thou say a *little*, even this, "I sat down under His shadow with *great delight*,

and His fruit was sweet to *my* taste"?
"What think ye of Christ?" Reader,
what dost thou think of Him? On thy
heart's honest answer to this question
eternity hangs. Leave doctrines and
creeds and Churches, and answer *this*,
"What dost *thou* think of Christ?

And mark, she tells us what Christ has
done for her. It is one of the first blessings the soul gets when it looks to Jesus.
—"I *sat* down." It is rest, wondrous rest,
perfect rest. It had roamed far and wide
in its search after this rest before, it had
drunk deep of every stream, but rest it
had never found. Now its eyes are open,
and it reads over each and all of these
streams, "whosoever drinketh of this water shall thirst again." Now it experiences the truth of another—"whosoever
drinketh of the water that I shall give
him shall *never* thirst." Ah! the world
has no rest to give. It never had. It
chafes and excites, it dazzles and wearies,
it stimulates and depresses; but this is
not rest. There is no rest apart from
Jesus. The heart must know Him, and

then it will "*sit* down." Then it rests, for it is in the "shadow" of Jesus. Then its heart experiences "great delight," for heaven's joy has entered into it.

But if there is rest, there is also *humility* implied in this figure. "Sitting down," we take the *low* place. "Sitting down," we are in the place of the *learner*, of the true disciple. Oh, what lessons we learn in that sweet resting-place at the feet of Jesus! Now we see how ignorant we are, and how much we have to learn. Now we have caught the mind of the seraphim—with four out of six wings we *cover* ourselves. We are in God's presence. We feel it. All is humility. Now the Spirit teaches us needed lessons about *ourselves* and about Jesus. He takes of the things of Christ, and shows them unto us. We eat of His fruit, and it is "sweet to our taste." We feel, while thus resting in His shadow, while thus lying low at His feet, that we are in a "banqueting house." The heart's joy is full. Its cup runneth over. He has *brought* us to this banqueting house. Ah, yes, He *brought* us. My soul, never forget that! Thou wouldst never have *come*. It is Jesus that *brought* thee, it is Jesus that *keeps* thee, and will not let thee go. All is sovereign grace. Thou hast nothing to boast of. All thy boasting is of Jesus, and must be throughout eternity—Jesus, and Jesus only. One banner floats over thee—the banner of Jesu's love. Yes, this is conspicuous. Every eye may see it. Love in coming down to our sin-stained world to seek and to save the lost ones. Love inscribed over the crimson cross in the brightness of the sun, as He lay suffering, bleeding, dying. Love shone brightly in Him and in all He did. And this is now our banner. Love in dying for us, love in saving us, love in keeping us, love in providing for us and watching over us. Love is the brightest star in the firmament of grace—the deep, constant, abiding love of Jesus. Well may our song for ever be " unto Him that loved us, and washed us from our sins in His own blood, and hath made us kings and priests unto God and His Father; to

Him be glory and dominion for ever and ever." "He *brought* me to the banqueting house, and His banner over me was love."

Reader, see what is to be found in Jesus. Rest, humility, great delight, sweet fruit, a banqueting house, and love floating over them all—the banner of Jesus, for "God is love." Oh, come and taste of these rich fruits! Drink deep draughts from this well of living waters! *Stoop down* and drink. Be humble, and thus be like Christ. Let down thy empty vessel again and again at this inexhaustible spring, for "the well is deep." Let thy tent be ever pitched near to it, and draw from hence the living streams that shall make thee glad! Thus shalt thou draw water from these wells of salvation with joy. "Thy soul shall be satisfied with marrow and fatness, and thy mouth shall praise Him with joyful lips."

THE FULNESS OF JESUS. 19

I heard the voice of Jesus say,
  "Come unto me, and rest;
Lay down, thou weary one, lay down,
  Thy head upon my breast."
I came to Jesus as I was—
  Weary and worn and sad;
I found in Him a resting-place,
  And He has made me glad.

I heard the voice of Jesus say,
  "Behold, I freely give
The living water; thirsty one,
  Stoop down, and drink, and live."
I came to Jesus, and I drank
  Of that life-giving stream;
My thirst was quenched, my soul revived,
  And now I live in Him.

I heard the voice of Jesus say,
  "I am this dark world's light;
Look unto me, thy morn shall rise,
  And all thy day be bright."
I looked to Jesus, and I found
  In Him my Star, my Sun;
And in that light of life I'll walk,
  'Till travelling days are done.

              REV. H. BONAR.

CHAPTER III.

The Disease and its Remedy.

"Stay me with flagons, comfort me with apples: for I am sick of love." *Song of Sol.* ii. 5.

"I AM sick of love!" What a change has come over the soul! A cloud has for a brief moment cast its dark shadow over her joy. The salvation is there, but the joy of it is withheld. There is intense affection to the Saviour, but without the realized presence of its object. There is the deep yearning, the increasing attachment, and yet the heart is sick. Why is this? Because, through some secret cause it fails to realize the assurance of *returned affection*. How often is this the case with the soul! None but Jesus, is its deep inward cry, and yet peace is not felt. Everything is sickening. The heart's very religion is sickening. The dark shadow that broods over that heart is cast over everything. The soul is sick —" sick of love."

And is not this the experience of many? Has it not, at one time or another, been the experience of every child of God? Was there not something of the same deep feeling in the cry, "My God, my God, why hast thou forsaken me?" Is the sun always shining upon us? Has our spiritual horizon no passing clouds? Have we no April sky, no autumnal drooping, no wintry blast sweeping by? Has the glassy sea no tempest breaking rudely over it, no ripple agitating for a moment the calm beauteous stillness of its placid waters? Ah! we know little of the divine life if we think so. We have learned to little purpose. There is a school of trial whose threshold has yet been uncrossed by our hearts. True, the sun is always shining, but shadows come across it, and they are reflected in the depths of our hearts. So long as the eye is on Jesus there is no cloud, no shadow, no passing vapour. All is brightness. It is "a morning without clouds."

And where do these clouds come from? From the sun? Nay, but from the earth. Not from above, but from below. Not from Jesus, but from our own hearts. The heart sends forth its mists and fogs and vapours, and thus the current of our peace is interrupted. The Lord Jesus is hidden. Dreariness and desolation are within. The heart is sick.

And what is the remedy? The heart breathes forth its prayer, "Restore unto me the joy of thy salvation"—"stay me with flagons"—bring to my thirsty lips the *heavenly vessels*. Bring to me the living waters in the vessels of the kingdom. "Comfort me with apples"—spread around me the *fruits of heaven*. Bring to my soul the fruit so sweet to my taste, so fragrant to my heart. This is the remedy—the vessels of living water, the fruits of the tree of life. It is simply Jesus in all His grace and love —Jesus as He is revealed in the word —Jesus as the Spirit of God presents

Him, through that word, to the soul. Who so fragrant to the believer as He? What so refreshing to the heart as the living water which flows down from Him? He is the fruit, and He the water, while the word of God, and those who minister that word in power and in truth to the soul, are the heavenly flagons. These are the "stay" and "comfort" of the drooping one. Used by the Spirit of God, the great Comforter of the Church, they are mighty. The soul revives. The shadows disappear. The heart's darkness vanishes like morning mists under the influence of the sun. It is once more bright and glad and happy. It has caught the smile of the Saviour, and goes on its way rejoicing. It realizes His love. It enjoys His presence. Its language is not now, "I am sick of love," but, "His left hand is under my head, and His right hand doth embrace me."

Reader do you know anything of this experience? Have shadows often crossed your soul? Has the light of heaven sometimes seemed darkness? Why is it? Has your Saviour changed? Has He hidden His countenance? Oh never, never! There are shadows everywhere, —above, around, below—but none *there*. Oh, none! The sunshine of His love never had a shadow yet and never will. As soon could yonder glorious sun emit from its bosom a mist, as that sweet countenance ever have a shadow towards thee. "Having loved His own which were in the world, He loved them to the end,"—or, as it means, "*through all*." He saw what thou *wast*, yet He loved thee. He saw what thou *wouldst* be, yet He loved thee. He saw thee a sinner, and saw thee a saint; He saw thee crooked and guilty, cold, unbelieving, and unworthy, yet He loved thee. He loved thee *through* it all. He loved thee, and will never cease to love thee. "Can a woman forget her sucking child? Yea, she may forget"—a case so unnatural may be— "yet will not I forget thee." "Thou art graven on the palms of my hands; thy walls are continually before me."

How has that darkness then come over

thy soul? Its cause may be physical. We are poor weak creatures. A change in the weather, the hearty enjoyment of a meal, some mental or nervous irritation, some unlooked-for intelligence,—these, and a thousand similar causes, may produce physical disorganization. Trust Him, believer, trust Him. Jesus changeth not though thou art changing every hour. Wait on the Lord. Keep the eye on Jesus. Rest in Him as revealed in His word, and peace will again flow into thy soul.

But what has that darkness sprung from? From a cause more serious. How did you get peace with God at first? You came to Jesus — just as you were, in all your sins, and looking to His precious blood, His finished work on Calvary, you found peace. Now, perhaps, your eye is off Him. You are looking at yourself — looking *in* at your heart instead of *out* at Jesus. No wonder you are unhappy. You found peace at first by looking to Jesus, and if you want to preserve that peace, it must be by looking to Jesus still. You *began* by looking away from yourself, you must *continue* by looking away from yourself. You began by looking to Jesus, you must continue by looking to Jesus. If you are looking at your heart, and wondering it does not improve, no wonder you are miserable. If you are expecting your prayers to be better, your faith to be stronger, your motives to be purer, your conduct to be holier, no wonder you have lost your peace. You have got your eye off Jesus. Look at yourself, not for peace, but for misery. Look at yourself, not to be satisfied with yourself, but to loathe yourself. Look at yourself if you will, to be driven away from yourself to Jesus. The eye off Jesus, and all is misery. The eye off Jesus, and shadows and darkness must wrap the soul. The eye off Jesus, no matter to what else turned, and the soul is in prison. It will heave and toss on its troubled waves and find no rest. No sound will be heard in its silent depths but the sound of the muffled drum—the deep, dark feeling of desolation and sorrow, of misery, despair, and death. Oh, look to Jesus! There alone is rest for the soul. There alone is peace for a troubled conscience. Look to Jesus, and *keep* looking to Jesus. Begin there, continue there, end there.

But what has that darkness sprung from? A cause more serious still—sin. Ah! no wonder you are miserable. You could scarcely be a child of God if sin gave you no uneasiness. If you could sit down easily with this, then indeed would Satan have fast hold of his prey. If the conscience is troubled, there is hope. If conscience is at rest, then is the soul asleep—yea "dead in trespasses and sins." If there is sin allowed, God must, God will, chasten. If we have no chastisement we are no children—we are "bastards and not sons." Thank God for chastisement! It shows us that we are His, and that He is determined to make us quit of sin and to make us like Himself.

Perhaps this is the secret cause of your darkness of mind—your deadness of spirit, your want of peace. You are indulging some secret sin, gratifying some secret but forbidden propensity. Perhaps the eye is unguarded, the thought unchecked, the imagination unrestrained. Perhaps the tongue, or the temper, or the disposition is not under the government of God's Holy Spirit. Perhaps there is some compromise with the world, the flesh, or the devil; a shrinking from taking up the cross; a hesitation in your testimony for Christ before men, from fear of being thought extreme, or from fear of losing their good opinion. Ah! these may be the secret cause of the darkness between your soul and God, your loss of peace, your want of assurance. There may be in the soul of many a child of God a secret process of declension going on, while there is nothing outwardly to mark it. There may be no outward inconsistency, no flaw in the moral conduct, nothing that the keenest eye can detect. The soul may be shaping its course so as to meet the eye of man or the eye of the Church, while all within is darkness deterioration and decay,—pardon gone, peace gone, joy gone, and communion with God kept up in form only, while the life, the spirit, the power of that communion which it once enjoyed, has long since departed. Can any state be more deplorable, more miserable? Yet may it not be—is it not actually—the state of multitudes of God's people? Oh, if we could only tear aside the flimsy covering which conceals the true state of the soul, what a melancholy picture would be disclosed! How many a Christian's heart should we find in a state of starvation, practically alienated from God? O Christian, be watchful! The snares of Satan lie thickly in your path. "Watch and pray, lest ye enter into temptation." Nothing so hides the Saviour from your soul as allowed sin or unwatchfulness of conduct. Remember that though your salvation is altogether the work of *another* —the Lord Jesus on the cross—your enjoyment of that salvation is dependent on *yourself*—on your obedient walk, your watchful conduct, your decision in all things for Christ. Oh watch, watch, watch!—watch unto prayer, watch against the flesh, watch against the world! If you be overtaken in sin, go at once to the blood. Wash in the blood at all times. Let not delay fester the wound, harden the heart, sear the conscience, draw a veil between the soul and God, and drag you down the world's broad, rapid, destructive stream. Live near to God. Then the heart will not be sick, but its language will be the joyous language of this song, "His left hand is under my head, and His right hand doth embrace me."

> "Ah! with such strange sights around me,
>   Fairest of what earth calls fair,—
> How I need thy fairer image,
>   To undo the syren snare!
> Lest the subtle serpent-tempter
>   Snare me with his radiant lie;
> As if sin were sin no longer,
>   Life no more a vanity.
>   Heir of glory,
> What is that to thee and me?

Yes, I need *thee*, heavenly city,
  My low spirit to upbear;
Yes, I need thee—earth's enchantments
  So beguile me with their glare.
Let me see thee—then these fetters
  Burst asunder—I am free;
Then this pomp no longer chains me—
  Faith has won the victory.
    Heir of glory,
  That shall be for thee and me.

Soon where earthly beauty blinds not,
  No excess of brilliance palls,
Salem, city of the holy,
  We shall be within thy walls!
There beside yon crystal river,
  There beneath life's healing tree,
There with nought to cloud or sever—
  Ever with the Lamb to be!
    Heir of glory,
  That shall be for thee and me!"

Rev. H. Bonar.

CHAPTER IV.

Our Place and its Blessings.

"His left hand is under my head, and his right hand doth embrace me. I charge you, O ye daughters of Jerusalem, by the roes, and by the hinds of the field, that ye stir not up, nor awake my love, till He please. The voice of my Beloved! behold, He cometh leaping upon the mountains, skipping upon the hills." *Song of Sol.* ii. 6–8.

"HIS left hand is under my head, and His right hand doth embrace me." Joy is now restored. The one who was "sick of love" is now in her right place. The cloud has passed over. The sunshine of heaven again shines brightly. The eye is on Jesus. His nearness is realized. His presence is sustaining her. His love is embracing her on every side. All is well.

The place she is now in is the right place. It is the place in which God would have all His children to be. For what is it? It is *nearness to Jesus, dwelling in His love*, and *leaning on His arm.* These are the three beautiful features implied in these words. Mark them, dear Christian reader, and you will see where God would have *you* to be. For what does He say to her in this place? "I charge you, O ye daughters of Jerusalem, by the roes and by the hinds of the field, that ye stir not up, nor awake my love, till He please," or, as it is more correctly rendered, "till *she* please." It is as if He would say to her, "This is your right place, your happy place, your safe place. Let not the world stir you from it. Let nothing draw you away from this spot." But the closing words confirm this view—"till *she* please," or, "till the hour of her *full pleasure* is come." And when will be the Church's hour of full pleasure? In the morning of resurrection. Thus she anticipates it: "I shall be *satisfied* when I *awake* with Thy likeness." That morning will be to her the fulness of joy. Then she will enter into the "pleasures for evermore," which are at her Saviour's right hand. Till that hour arrive, her place is to be with His left hand under her head, and His right hand embracing her,—near to Jesus, leaning upon Him, and dwelling in His love.

We see how clearly this is the place God would have us be in, from the solemn manner in which the Lord enjoins it— "I *charge* you." It is the counterpart of the Saviour's frequently reiterated words, "*Abide* in me, and I in you;" or of the beloved Apostle John, "and now, little children, *abide* in Him;" "he that *abideth* in Him sinneth not;" "he that abideth in Him ought himself so to walk even as He walked."

And what a *safe* place for the soul! What a sweet, happy, holy spot! How spiritually alive it is kept there! How is spiritual discernment and perception deepened! What holy sensitiveness characterizes it! How quick it becomes to recognise God's ways, hear God's voice, trace God's footsteps, discern God's image wherever it is to be seen! How remarkably this is conveyed in the figure the Holy Spirit employs in these words—"I charge you, by *the roes, and by the hinds of the field.*" How quickly alive above all others these animals are to the least approach of danger. The slightest sound can be heard by them at great distances. That which would be unheard by any other animal is heard most clearly and distinctly by the roe and the hind. Most expressive figure! The soul that is living near to Jesus, leaning on Him, and dwelling in His love, will surely be in a safe place. It will be alive to the least approach of spiritual danger. What is unseen and unheard by other Christians, because of spiritual obtuseness, will be quickly seen and heard by it. It will discern most quickly the Lord's mind, the Lord's ways, the Lord's image everywhere. Do we not see this manifested in some Christians in a very marked manner? One who is living near to Jesus and in some path of doubt or perplexity, difficulty or danger, with, perhaps, no clear command before him in the word of

God how to act, yet discovers the *spirit* of that word, and acts upon it. He discerns the Lord's mind more by spiritual intuition than by any direct command. Another, living more at a distance from the Saviour, needs a plain command, and without it cannot act at all, or acts wrongly. The one has its type in Abraham, the other in Lot. Both are true men, but one lives near to God, and chooses by faith, the other is living at a distance, and walks by sight. The one chooses the wilderness — God's place, because he recognises God's mind; the other chooses the "well watered plains," the place of danger and sorrow and sin.

Take another case, equally remarkable, and corroborative of this truth. We find it in the twenty-first chapter of St. John's Gospel. Who was it that lived *near to Jesus, leaned on His bosom*, and *dwelt in His love*,—so dwelt in His love as to make it a *hiding*-place, not allowing *his own name* to be mentioned, save as " the disciple whom Jesus loved "? It was the beloved John. Mark the contrast between him and Peter here. Who was the first among the whole band of disciples to perceive the Lord on the shore? Even this same disciple (ver. 7). Again (vers. 19, 20), Peter needs a *command* to follow Jesus; not only so, but needs that command to be *repeated* before he can act upon it. But the one who was living near to Jesus, who leaned on Him, and dwelt in His love, is seen following *without a command.* Thus it will be always. Nearness to Jesus is our sweetest, safest place. Living near Him, we shall not go far wrong. We shall see *our* way where others stumble. We shall recognise the Lord's image where another will only see nature or the flesh. We shall be safe, because near; happy, because dwelling in His love; strong, because leaning on His arm.

We have an evidence of the truth of these remarks in the opening clause of the eighth verse: "The voice of my Beloved!" are the words she utters from this place of nearness to Jesus. The

Lord had just spoken. She quickly heard His voice. She heard it because she was near. The spiritual ear is opened, and, like Mary at the sepulchre, there is a joyful recognition of Him she loves; or, like the beloved disciple on the shore of Tiberias, "It is the Lord!" The heart leaps up at the sound of His voice or at the recognition of His person. "My sheep hear my voice," is the mark the Shepherd Himself has given us of those who are His. It is this voice they seek to hear wherever they go. "A stranger will they not follow, for they know not the voice of strangers."

But let us mark another beautiful truth presented in this verse. From this place of nearness to Jesus she casts her eye forward to the coming of the Lord. "The voice of my Beloved! behold, He cometh leaping upon the mountains, skipping upon the hills." We have here the unvarying preface to that event so frequently mentioned in the New Testament: "Behold He cometh;" "*Behold, He cometh* with clouds; and every eye shall see Him;" "*behold, I come* quickly." So with the Church here. Living near to Jesus, we realize most vividly the coming of the Lord. The eye rests not on anything between, but passes on with a bound to the glories of that day. It is only when we are in the place she was here, " His left hand under her head, and His right hand embracing her," that the coming of the Lord becomes a *practical* thing—a living principle in the soul. Let us be in any other place we may, and this glorious truth must degenerate into a doctrine, a subject of discussion, the badge of a party, and be without any real power in the soul. But living near to Jesus, leaning on His arm, dwelling in His love,—oh what a power there is in it, what a Divine reality it becomes! We hear the Shepherd's voice, and our hearts leap up with joy as we exclaim, " Behold, He cometh! "

And this is the end for which the Church is chosen. From the moment she is brought to know Jesus, she has to wait for " that blessed hope." Faith from that moment transports her into that day.

Her home is there, not here. Her joys are there, not here. Her heart is there, not here. "To wait for His Son from heaven," was whispered in her ear by the Spirit of God, from the moment she was brought to the Saviour. And just as she lives near to Jesus, she will live in that day. Like the loved one here, she will not say, "Behold, He *will* come;" but, "behold, He *cometh*." To her there is nothing to intervene. She is *in* that day now. She is a child of the morning—"the morning without clouds." It is the "blessed hope" set before her that makes all things light here. It is the morning glories which surround her, and which make her "light afflictions but for a moment." She is looking at the things unseen and eternal. The morning sun is already gilding the distant hills, and she is putting on her garments of glory to accompany the King. All is joy; all is glory; all is radiant with bliss—and all because she is living near to Jesus.

But in what a triumphant light is the

coming of the Lord set before us here. "Behold, He cometh leaping upon the mountains, skipping upon the hills." "Leaping," joyfully anticipating that great event. Oh, if the prospect be joyous to us, how much more to Him! He is longing for that hour when He shall clasp to His bosom His purchased, blood-bought Bride. Again and again does He repeat it, as if to assure her and encourage her, "Surely I come quickly!" Thus is He brought before us as leaping, in joyful anticipation of that hour; "skipping upon the hills," or as it would imply in the original, "with his legs contracted"—ready to make a *bound*. Such is the delightful attitude in which the Lord Jesus is set before us in relation to that day.

But He comes in triumphant majesty. "leaping upon the *mountains*, skipping upon the *hills*." The mountains and hills of this earth of ours are formed by the *convulsions of nature*. The Lord is represented as coming to reign, having all these convulsions under His feet. All the mountains of sin and evil, of discord and division, all those mountains of ungodliness which have been thrown up by the convulsions in the world and the Church, thrown up by man's sin and the Church's weakness,— these are now all under His feet. He is the great Restorer. The crooked places shall be made straight. The mountain shall become a plain. He shall be "King of kings and Lord of lords," and "the Lord alone shall be exalted in that day." Yes, great and numerous as are the mountains and hills of sin and evil around, there is One on high greater than them all. He has them all under His feet. "The Lord sitteth on the water-flood: the Lord remaineth King for ever." Precious thought! strong consolation! as we see sin increasing on every side, "the love of many waxing cold, and men's hearts failing them for fear, looking after those things that are coming on the earth."

Reader, be ready for that hour. How can you best be so? Live near to Jesus, lean on His bosom, dwell in His love.

From that holy, sweet spot you will be quick to hear your Saviour's voice, and strong to do His will. You will have around your soul a Divine panoply against danger: and when the Lord Jesus shall cleave asunder the clouds of heaven to summon you to Himself, your waiting spirit shall catch the sound of His glad welcome, and exclaim, " The voice of my Beloved! behold, He cometh leaping upon the mountains, skipping upon the hills."

" Soon—and for ever!"
    Such promise our trust,
Though ashes to ashes,
    And dust unto dust;
Soon—and for ever
    Our union shall be
Made perfect, our glorious
    Redeemer, in Thee.
When the sin and the sorrows
    Of time shall be o'er;
Its pangs and its partings
    Remembered no more;

THE CHANGED ONES.

When life cannot fail,
 And when death cannot sever;
Christians with Christ shall be
 Soon—and for ever.

Soon—and for ever
 The breaking of day
Shall drive all the night-clouds
 Of sorrow away.
Soon—and for ever
 We'll see as we're seen,
And learn the true meaning
 Of things that have been.
When fightings without us,
 And fears from within,
Shall weary no more
 In the warfare of sin.
Where tears and where fears,
 And where death shall be never;
Christians with Christ shall be
 Soon—and for ever.

Soon—and for ever
 The work shall be done,
The warfare accomplished,
 The victory won.
Soon—and for ever,
 The soldier lay down
His sword for a harp,
 And his cross for a crown.

Then droop not in sorrow,
　　Despond not in fear,
A glorious to-morrow
　　Is brightening and near;
When—blessed reward
　　Of each faithful endeavour—
Christians with Christ shall be
　　Soon—and for ever."

CHAPTER V

The Church beholding Christ.

"My Beloved is like a roe or a young hart: behold, He standeth behind our wall, He looketh forth at the windows, showing Himself through the lattice." *Song of Sol.* ii. 9.

WE have in these expressive words the Church beholding the Lord. He is compared here to a roe and a young hart. These figures, taken as they stand in this passage, are significant and instructive. We find (Deut. xiv. 5; xii. 15) that the roe was the emblem of purity and grace. It was (xv. 22) food for clean and unclean, saint and sinner. In this it fitly represents the purity and grace of the Lord Jesus, and of His character as the food of all who come to Him—"the living bread sent down from heaven."

But the most important aspect of it is in its representation of the Lord Jesus in His coming glory. The meaning of the "roe" is the *beautiful one*. It was not permitted to be offered in sacrifice, and, consequently, could not typify Christ as the sin-offering. It therefore stands before us a fit emblem of the Lord Jesus when He shall come "the second time without sin unto salvation,"—the Lord Jesus in His glory and beauty, as we shall behold Him in the morning of resurrection.

The use of the word in other parts of Scripture confirms this view. Where the word "beauty," or "glory," is used, it is the same word as is rendered "roe" in this passage. "In that day shall the Lord of hosts be for a crown of glory, and for a diadem of beauty, unto the residue of His people" (Isa. xxviii. 5). "In the day that I lifted up mine hand unto them, to bring them forth of the land of Egypt into a land that I had espied for them, flowing with milk and honey, which is the glory of all lands" (Ezek. xx. 6).

"The beauty of Israel is slain." In these and other parts of Scripture the words rendered "glory" and "beauty" are the same as that which is rendered "roe" in this passage.

Also with reference to the second figure under which the Lord Jesus is presented to us in this passage—the young hart, the meaning is equally significant and instructive. The "hart," or *strong one*, is the figure under which He is presented to us in other parts of God's word. In the 22nd Psalm we find the dedication to "aijeleth shahar"—"the hind of the morning," or "*the morning strong one.*" It is from the same root we derive "the mighty power of God."

We have the Lord Jesus thus brought before us under the figures of the "roe" and "young hart," as the glorious and beautiful one, the morning strong one. The Church beholds Him *now* as such. She casts her eye forward to that hour, and sees Him, all glory, beauty, and strength, coming to take His people to Himself, "to be admired in all them that believe," to be the strong one to crush Antichrist and his hosts, and to give power to His weak, down-trodden people Israel. It is thus He is brought before us in the psalm I have quoted; and therefore the dedication to "the hind of the morning," or "the morning strong one."

But where does the Church behold Him now? "Behold He standeth behind our wall." "He *standeth*"—at the right hand of the Father; "ever living to make intercession for us." "Behind our wall;" the Church has a *protection* thrown around her. She is within an enclosure. She is "kept by the power of God unto salvation." On the other side of this wall stands the Lord Jesus, at the Father's throne, on our behalf.

But though there is a wall between us and the Saviour, there are "windows" through which He looks down upon us, and through which we see and speak with Him. These "windows" let in the light and atmosphere of heaven. What more fit and beautiful representation of the Holy Spirit, the word of God, and the ministry of that word in the Church! These are its "windows," through which the light and atmosphere of heaven come down to our souls. Through these we see Jesus, and hold fellowship with Him. Through these He speaks to us, and we listen to His voice. Through that blessed word He "flourishes Himself through the lattice"—*shews Himself in all His parts*. If we want to know Him and to hear His voice, we must look through "the windows," we must come to "the lattice." Only there does He reveal Himself. We may see much of God in nature, and God's natural laws may be acknowledged by the conscience; but He who would see Jesus and know Him must come to the word of God, and be taught by His Spirit. Without this, man's boasted light is darkness itself. He knows not God as revealed in the Lord Jesus, and therefore the highest point to which his religion culminates is that of "the unknown God." The nation of all others the most polished, the most refined, the most artistic, the most learned—so much so that everything Greek or Grecian is the model in our universities and schools of art at this very day—was the nation that raised this altar. Athens, in all her grandeur, could soar no higher than this. Oh! convincing testimony, to every thoughtful mind, of the poverty of everything to enlighten and save man without the knowledge of Jesus! How ignorant, how blind, how wretched the soul in the midst of everything of which a nation might justly be proud! Ah! man needs the word of God and the Spirit of God to enlighten him. He needs the blood to make an atonement for his soul. He needs Jesus to lift him up from death and darkness and ruin to life and light and immortality. These are themes which Athens in all her grandeur never knew, of which none of her proud philosophers could boast, but which are the everlasting inheritance of every sinner who trusts in Jesus.

Reader, prize these blessed privileges. Remember how much greater is your responsibility in consequence, and "how much sorer" the condemnation if lightly esteemed. Clasp the word of God to your heart as your choicest treasure. Come to "the windows" and "the lattice," and there behold your Saviour. Let nothing tempt you to a hurried meeting— a few passing words with Him. Take trouble about your Bible. Meditate and pray over it much. Seek its guidance in everything, and have no fellowship with anything that has not its clear sanction. Take your stand by it at all times—with Christ in the one hand and your precious Bible in the other. Let these be inseparable, and accompany you through life. Thus will you be preserved in the midst of danger, and light clear and bright will shine upon your path till you enter within the gates of the heavenly Jerusalem. "Hold that fast which thou hast, that no man take thy crown."

"Jesus! how much Thy name unfolds
  To every opened ear;
The pardoned sinner's memory holds
  None other half so dear.

Jesus ! it speaks a life of love,
   And sorrows meekly borne ;
It tells of sympathy above,
   Whatever sins we mourn.

It tells us of Thy sinless walk
   In fellowship with God ;
And, to our ears, no tale so sweet
   As Thine atoning blood.

This name encircles every grace
   That God as man could show ;
There only can the Spirit trace
   A perfect life below.

The mention of Thy name shall bow
   Our hearts to worship Thee ;
The chiefest of ten thousand Thou,
   The chief of sinners we."

CHAPTER VI.

The Exhortation and Motive.

"My Beloved spake, and said unto me, Rise up, my love, my fair one, and come away. For, lo, the winter is past, the rain is over and gone; the flowers appear on the earth; the time of the singing *of birds* is come, and the voice of the turtle is heard in our land; the fig tree putteth forth her green figs, and the vines with the tender grape give a good smell. Arise, my love, my fair one, and come away." *Song of Sol.* ii. 10–13.

THERE is no subject in God's word more practical than the second coming of the Lord Jesus Christ. Yet how often are we asked the question, "Of what *practical* use is it?" Surely such people have read the New Testament, especially the epistles of it, very superficially or to very little purpose, if they do not see that almost every injunction to holiness of life and separation from the present evil world has for its great motive " *the*

Lord is at hand." It is because this glorious truth has become a *doctrine* rather than a *living principle in the soul* that such questions have arisen, and that there prevails such unbelief on the subject. What, we would ask, could keep us more separate from the world, more sober, watchful, holy, than the conviction deeply rooted within, that the Lord may be here before nightfall? And this is the way in which it is ever set before us in the Bible—"Watch ye *therefore*, for ye know neither the day nor the hour the Son of man cometh." Mark how it is thus used elsewhere—"When Christ, who is our life, shall *appear*, then shall ye also appear with Him in glory" (Col. iii. 4, 5). What follows from this motive?—"Mortify, *therefore*, your members which are upon the earth."

It is thus set before us in the beautiful portion of God's word we are about to consider. The Lord speaks to His Church in anticipation of that glorious hour—"The winter is past"—the coldness and dreariness and desolation of this dark night of sin and iniquity—the time of withering and blight, when resurrection life is a hidden thing, like spring sap in the tree—all this is past. "The rain is over and gone"—God's judgments have been poured out on the wicked. "The flowers appear on the earth"—the evidence that the resurrection morning has arrived with all its fragrance and beauty. "The time of the singing is come" ("of birds" is not in the original)—the time of the singing of the "new song" by "a multitude which no man can number." "The voice of the turtle is heard in our land"—the appearance of the summer bird telling us that summer is *indeed* come. "The fig-tree putteth forth her figs"— the fig-tree, or Jewish nation, just beginning to bring forth fruit to God. "The vines and the tender grapes give a good smell"—the Jewish nation and the land of Israel bringing forth fruits fragrant and well-pleasing to God, being *now* offered through Jesus Christ their accepted King. This is the glorious anticipation which the Lord sets before His people *as a mo-*

tive. What is the practical tendency of it? Separation from the world, holiness of life—"*arise,* my love, my fair one, and *come away.*" How clearly we see all through God's word that there is in it no motive more practical than the glorious truth that the Lord Jesus is at hand! "*Behold,* I come quickly." "*Surely* I come quickly!" Reader, may your heart and mine respond, "Even so, come, Lord Jesus; come quickly."

But observe how this passage is introduced. "My Beloved *spake* (or "*answered*"), and *said* unto me." This mode of expression has its correspondence in the New Testament. "Jesus *answered* and *said* unto them." There is no tautology here. The repetition is significant and instructive. There had been *no previous question* put, and yet she says "my beloved *answered* and said unto me." The simple explanation of this is, that what He *said* to her was the *answer* to her *heart,* to the *thoughts* passing then in her mind. It was the exact answer to the *need* of her soul. It is different with *us*. Our speaking is not always the *answer* to what is passing in the mind of another. In the Lord Jesus it was always so, for "He knew what was in man." He knew man as none else knew him. His speaking, therefore, was on all occasions exactly what the heart needed.

So is it in this passage. The Lord spake to her of the coming glory, of the glad and happy hour before her. This was not only the *answer* to her *need* (for surely the gladness of that time is what the Church and creation deeply needs) but it was the answer to her *heart*. It produced a *response*. It awakened her hopes, her joys, her gladness. Oh, how truly did the Lord *answer* when He spake to her of these glad tidings!

The endearing terms applied by the Lord to His people here is also instructive—"Rise up, my *love*, my *fair* one." He says "love" *first*. He could not have said "my *fair* one" unless He had *first* said "my *love*." "He *loved* us and gave Himself for us" first. Then, having washed all our sins away, we became "fair," we were "accepted in the beloved." We became then *as Christ Himself* before God. God looks at us in Jesus. And looked at *only in Jesus,* what other language *could* He use, sinners though we are, than this, "thou art *all* fair my love; there is *no spot* in thee." Precious Jesus! What guilty creatures *we* are! What wondrous love is Thine!

Reader, dost thou shrink back and exclaim, "this is too great!" Too great for *Him?* Away with such narrow-souled, contracted views of thy Saviour and His love! He is a *great* Saviour, and a *great* gift becomes Him. Thou wouldst lessen its greatness by thy narrow thoughts of it, with thy conditions, thy "ifs" and "buts" and "hopes" and "may be's." Give thy Saviour credit for generosity. Give Him credit for a generous gift, a *great* gift, worthy of Himself, even salvation to *thee,* just as thou art, in all thy sin. This is worthy of Him. If thy thoughts, or thy faith, or thy prayers, or thy deeds could do anything to merit that gift, would not the greatness of it be lessened and also the generosity of the giver? What would awaken in the breast of a criminal feelings of devotion and gratitude to his king? A *free, undeserved* pardon. This would be a *generous* gift. What if the criminal should say, "It will place me under too great a debt to the king's goodness. I will do something to *earn* it, so that I shall not feel under so great an obligation"? Would not this be *pride?* Would not this make the king less a *giver*, and the criminal more an *earner?* Would not this lessen the greatness of the king's *gift*, reduce the idea of his *generosity*, and make any feelings of gratitude or devotion in the criminal's bosom *less intense?* Ah! sinner, see in this picture thyself. What a generous gift Christ offers thee! Salvation *now*, just as thou art! What a noble gift! How worthy of Him! How will this waken feelings of devotion and love to Him for such a gift to thee, a poor hell-deserving sinner! But what art thou saying? "It is too great, too good, I cannot believe it." Oh, take this generous gift from a generous Giver, and let thy thoughts of Him be great—thoughts of such love, such mercy, such grace, such goodness! Dismiss for ever the dishonouring idea of making yourself *more worthy*, and so making it less a gift on God's part to you, and making you more proud in the thought that you have *earned it*. Salvation is a great gift worthy of a great Saviour. Take this gift; take it *now;* take it as a guilty sinner; take it and glorify Him for such wondrous love to thee! Take it, sinner, a great and generous gift from a great and gracious Saviour. Then wilt thou hear His voice to thee, though a sinner, " thou art all fair, my love : there is no spot in thee." His will be throughout eternity the praise, and thine the rejoicing.

But mark the Lord's exhortation, "Rise up, my love, my fair one, and come away." " Rise up" out of sloth and slumber. " It is high time that we should awake out of sleep." " Awake thou that sleepest, and arise from the dead, and Christ shall give thee light." "Arise ye, and *depart*, for this is not your rest;" it is polluted.

> "We've no abiding city here,
> We seek a city out of sight;
> Zion its name, the Lord is there,
> It shines in everlasting light."

This is God's continued call—"rise up" out of sleep; "come away"—to that brighter and better land I have just been describing, where the winter is past and all its witherings, the rain and all its judgments, the weeds and all their poison, sin and all its discordant sounds, fruitlessness and all its attendant sorrows. Thus also He speaks in this same book—" come with me from the lions' dens and the mountains of leopards." It is as if He would say, "this world is the place of danger and death, the place of lions' dens and mountains of leopards; walk with me to a better inheritance; "come up out of the wilderness, leaning upon your Beloved;" "arise, my love, my fair one, and come away." And shall we not go with Him? O precious Saviour, "draw us, and we will run after Thee!" "Lord, to whom shall we go but to Thee?" "Whom have we in heaven but Thee? and there is none upon earth we desire in comparison of Thee. Our flesh and our heart faileth us; but Thou art the strength of our hearts, and our portion for ever."

Reader, walk with Jesus. Go with Him everywhere. Go not without Him anywhere. "Rise up" out of sloth and slumber and sleep, and be wakeful, watchful, vigilant. "Rise up" to *Him* in everything you have to do. Rise daily from self and sin, nearer and nearer to Him. "Onward and upward, heavenward and homeward," be this your motto and your aim through life. "Come away," is the Spirit's message ringing in your ears now more loudly than ever. "Come away," for this world is not your rest. "Come away," for it has rejected and crucified your Lord and Master, and judgment now awaits it for its crime. "Come away," for it is a place of death, a place of sighs and tears, a place of withering and blighting, of gloom and sadness and sorrow. "Come away,"—the voice of the Lord bids you. Every sound of the funeral bell utters the same cry. Every pang that shoots through the frame bids you. Every flower that lies withered at your feet bids you. Every storm that breaks over your head bids you. Every voice from heaven bids you. Every voice on earth bids you—"arise, and come away." Ye "loved ones" of the Lord Jesus, ye "fair ones," washed in His precious blood, hark to your Saviour's call! "The night is far spent, the day is at hand: let us cast off the works of darkness, and put upon us the armour of light. Let us walk honestly, as in the day; not in rioting and drunkenness, not in chambering and wantonness, not in strife and envying. But put ye on the Lord Jesus Christ, and make not provision for the flesh, to fulfil the lusts thereof."

" Where the faded flower shall freshen,—
Freshen never more to fade:
Where the shaded sky shall brighten,—
Brighten never more to shade;

Where the sun-blaze never scorches;
　　Where the star-beams cease to chill;
Where no tempest stirs the echoes
　　Of the wood, or wave, or hill:
Where the morn shall wake in gladness,
　　And the noon the joy prolong;
Where the daylight dies in fragrance,
　　'Mid the burst of holy song:
　　　　　Brother, we shall meet and rest
　　　　　'Mid the holy and the blest!

Where no shadow shall bewilder,
　　Where life's vain parade is o'er,
Where the sleep of sin is broken,
　　And the dreamer dreams no more:
Where the bond is never severed:—
　　Partings, claspings, sob and moan,
Midnight waking, twilight weeping,
　　Heavy noontide—all are done.
Where the child has found its mother,
　　Where the mother finds the child,
Where dear families are gathered,
　　That were scattered on the wild.
　　　　　Brother, we shall meet and rest
　　　　　'Mid the holy and the blest!

Where the hidden wound is healèd,
　　Where the blighted life reblooms,
Where the smitten heart the freshness
　　Of its buoyant youth resumes;

THE CHANGED ONES.

Where the love that here we lavish
   On the withering leaves of time,
Shall have fadeless flowers to fix on
   In an ever spring-bright clime,
Where we find the joy of loving,
   As we never loved before,—
Loving on, unchilled, unhindered,
   Loving once and evermore:
      Brother, we shall meet and rest
      'Mid the holy and the blest!

Where a blasted world shall brighten,
   Underneath a bluer sphere,
And a softer, gentler, sunshine
   Shed its healing splendour here;
Where earth's barren vales shall blossom,
   Putting on their robe of green,
And a purer, fairer Eden
   Be where only wastes have been:
Where a King in kingly glory,
   Such as earth has never known,
Shall assume the righteous sceptre,
   Claim and wear the holy crown:
      Brother, we shall meet and rest
      'Mid the holy and the blest!

                    REV. H. BONAR.

CHAPTER VII.

The Hiding-Place: its Blessings and Dangers.

"O my dove, that art in the clefts of the rock, in the secret places of the stairs, let me see thy countenance, let me hear thy voice; for sweet is thy voice, and thy countenance is comely. Take us the foxes, the little foxes, that spoil the vines: for our vines have tender grapes." *Song of Sol.* ii. 14, 15.

THE Lord is here speaking to His Church. The figure under which she is described is the embodiment of meekness, grace, gentleness, and love. It is that under which His Holy Spirit is presented to us in the word of God. And if the Lord's people be indeed found where the dove is seen here, then will the characteristics of the holy Dove be seen in them.

The characteristic feature of the dove is

that she has but *one* mate. So the Church has but one—Jesus. She knows no other. She wants no other. She is satisfied with Him, and without Him she has nothing. And as Jesus is all to her, so she is all to Him. " My dove, my undefiled is but *one*." He loved her and gave Himself for her. He has espoused her to Himself, and His delight is in her.

" O my dove "— my *oppressed* one. The fifty-sixth Psalm—" a *golden* Psalm of David "—has its dedication to "the dove's dumb one." She is called "the *golden* one" (Ps. lxviii. 13). She takes refuge far away from the haunts of men in some craggy rock (Jer. xlviii. 28). In the sides of this rock there are steps cut by which she has access to the fortress. This cleft, or craggy rock, has its secret place or covert where the dove securely takes shelter, and reposes in confidence (Ps. xxvii. 5 ; xxxii. 7 ; xci. 1).

This rock is Christ. He is called " the shadow of a great rock in a weary land." Still it is not *on* the Rock that the dove is seen, but *in* the Rock. We may have Christ in His life, Christ in His example, yea, Christ in His *love*, and yet be *lost*. We may be *on* the Rock so far, yet not be safe. The place of safety is *in* the Rock—in the *cleft* of that Rock—in other words, in a *crucified* Saviour. This is the danger of the present day. Very much is made in some sense of this Rock, but the *cleft* Rock is left out of sight. Men speak of Christ's humility, Christ's gentleness and meekness, Christ's love and mercy, but what of the blood? What of a *crucified* Saviour? "It is the *blood* that maketh atonement for the soul." "Without *shedding of blood* is no remission of sins." Men speak of the *love* of Jesus with the tongue of angels, and listening multitudes are captivated with their eloquence. All this time the *blood* is denied. A *crucified* Saviour is ignored. Their hearers have been drinking in the most deadly poison. The subtle error—the soul-destroying *omission*—is undetected by the mass, and the poor ignorant crowd, blinded by the dazzling eloquence of the preacher, and by the proclamation of *one side* only of the truth, go on in darkness and error and sin. The Rock is there, but no *hiding-place* for the poor storm-beaten dove. Jesus is there, but no riven side in which sinners may hide under the impending wrath of a just and holy God. No blood to wash away their guilty stains. No Saviour having atoned for the breach of a broken law, in whom the sinner may stand "all fair and spotless" at the great and terrible day! O miserable theology, soul-destroying system of error, possessing no drop of balm for the sin-convicted conscience, but to leave it out crying out in agony unmitigated, "O wretched man that I am! who shall deliver me from the body of this death!" No, poor, agonizing one; the dead body of sin must cling to thee! There is no hope! Thou must drag that heavy load through life! It must weigh heavier and heavier till thou sink beneath its mountain-weight!

And this is the theology that is now beginning to be fashionable! This is the system that is beginning to be caressed by the *intellect* of the day! A Saviour without the cross! A Saviour without the blood! This is "rational" religion! This is the system *intellect* boasts of, education endorses, and which dazzles even royalty itself! Blessed be God for His holy, precious word! There is a Physician—there is balm in Gilead! There is a *cleft* in the Rock where the conscience-stricken soul may hide in peace, where the dove may take refuge from the storm that is raging around her. That Rock is Jesus. That cleft is His riven side—the precious blood that "cleanseth from all sin." There is refuge. There is peace. There is rest. There is sunshine in the midst of gloom, light in the midst of darkness, joy in the midst of sorrow, yea, heaven even on earth. There the burden falls into the tomb, and the soul, its fetters burst asunder, leaps up in joy and gladness.

Blessed be God for the cleft in the Rock where the oppressed dove may hide. What *could* we do without it? Oh, may our hearts ever respond to words that have become a proverb in the Church,—

"Rock of ages, cleft for me,
Let me hide myself in Thee;
Let the water and the blood,
From Thy riven side which flowed,
Be of sin the double cure,
Cleanse me from its guilt and power."

Mark, reader, a solemn lesson. Where does God speak these gracious, loving words to His people? In the cleft of the Rock. If we want to hear God speaking words of peace and love to our souls, it is there we must hide. When Moses heard words from God of the same gracious character, where did he hear them? Even in the cleft of the rock where God had hidden him. So must it ever be with us. There, and only there, shall we learn God's true character. There, and only there, the sweet notes of pardoning mercy, of acceptance in the Beloved, of union with Jesus can be heard. This is God's resting-place for the oppressed dove. This is the sweetest spot on this side heaven. Make *much* of it, dear Christian reader; and may you be found there at all times!

But the dove has her "secret" in that

cleft. Even so, those who hide in a crucified Saviour have their "secret place" in Him. "The secret of the Lord is with them that fear Him." What sweet meeting-places with their heavenly Father! What whispers to their souls! What nearness to Him they love! How do they sometimes seem to be "out of the body" there! How do they so vividly realize His presence, that they seem to be surrounded with the light of heaven! What special tokens of His love and care and watchfulness towards them they sometimes have! Ah! there are "secrets" in the "cleft Rock" which they alone know who are hiding there, and living near to Jesus.

In this hiding place the Lord speaks to His people in a *special* manner: "Let me see thy countenance; let me hear thy voice." The heart of the Saviour breathes over His loved ones with *intense* affection: "sweet is thy voice, and thy countenance is comely." What wondrous language to sinners such as we are! What amazing grace, as we think of the way in which we have treated Him since He drew us to Himself! What provocations of His 'love, what coldness of service, what deadness of soul, what selfishness and worldliness, what murmuring and thanklessness, and rebellion! Yet to us, as we *have been*, and as we *are*, He says, " *O my dove . . . let me see thy countenance, let me hear thy voice: for sweet is thy voice, and thy countenance is comely!* " Lord, what love is Thine! Surely not even eternity itself will be able to tell what *it* is! O wondrous love of Jesus! O precious Saviour, who dost love us so, keep us from dishonouring Thee by our sinful doubts; for " as far as the east is from the west," so far is Thy love above our *highest* thoughts of it!

Christian reader, live in the " cleft" and in " the secret place " of that Rock. Then wilt thou hear that dear Saviour telling out His love to thee. Live very near to Him. Let Him hear *thy* voice there. Let Him behold *thy* face. Let no cloud come between that bright countenance and thy soul. If it should, oh haste to the blood, haste to the blood, and all will be bright again.

But now we have had the blessings of "the cleft rock," and its "secret place," let us notice the dangers. "Take us the foxes, the little foxes, that spoil the vines: for our vines have tender grapes." Great spiritual blessings are not unfrequently fore-runners of great spiritual trials. They are the preparation for them. The lifting up into the third heaven, and being permitted to see unspeakable things, was followed by "the thorn in the flesh," for which these spiritual blessings were the preparation. So also in the case of our blessed Lord Himself. The opened heavens, the Father's voice, the unclouded sunshine falling upon Him (Mark i.), were followed by the wilderness, Satan, and the wild beasts. There are numerous instances of a similar kind in the New Testament confirming this. So is it here. The bride had been holding secret fellowship with her Beloved in "the cleft of the rock, in the secret place of the stairs." He had made known to her the depths of

His love in the words, "Let me see thy countenance, let me hear thy voice; for sweet is thy voice, and thy countenance is comely." These were great spiritual enjoyments, special manifestations of the Lord's love to her soul. They were also the preparation-work for what He is now about to make known to her. He warns her of danger. It is alongside of her, yea, on the very border of these spiritual enjoyments. "Take us the foxes, the little foxes, that spoil the vines." Real spiritual danger and true spiritual privilege ever run alongside of each other. Christian reader, never forget this. If we search the word, we shall find that when the Lord's people have made some slip in their path, it has invariably been after great spiritual privilege and enjoyment. Abraham, Moses, Elijah, David, are all instances of this. At such seasons the child of God is more likely to be off his guard. There Satan watches and trips up the incautious Christian. Never do we need to be more watchful than in seasons of great spiritual joy or spiritual privilege, such as the bride had enjoyed here. Never do we need the warning, "watch and pray," "take unto you the *whole* armour of God," more than at such a moment. For when is it that the foxes make their appearance among the vines? Not in the dreariness and desolation of winter, when the vine-tree is stripped of its foliage, and apparently a lifeless stem. No, but in summer, when the foliage of the vine-tree is thick and beautiful, when the vines begin to bear, and when all around betokens summer fruitfulness. Then do the foxes, yea the *little* foxes, move stealthily among the rich foliage, and inserting their teeth in the bark of the vine-stock, cast a withering blight over the once beautiful tree. Oh my soul, learn the instructive lesson, the solemn warning, the Spirit of God would teach thee! When all is summer with thy soul, when all is joy and gladness within thee, when thy Lord has whispered in thine ear, "O *my* dove, sweet is thy voice, and thy countenance is comely," then "watch thou in all things." Danger is near. The little foxes are not far distant. "Put on the *whole* armour of God." Leave no part of thy soul unclothed. Leave no path, no way of thine, unwatched. Hide deeper in the cleft of the Rock of ages. Keep very near to Jesus. Oh, it is then, when thy soul is enjoying secret communion with the Saviour, that "the vines have tender grapes." What a tender, sensitive plant is the Spirit of God within thee! What a little thing, like the "little fox," will draw a veil between thee and Jesus! What a little thing will draw over thy soul a cloud, a vapour, or a film, shading the brightness of His countenance, and making the heart droop with sadness! A thought, an imagination, a look, a word, a temper, an act not *altogether* straightforward,—oh these "little foxes," how they spoil the vines, how they blight the tender grapes! Watch, Christian, watch! Be on thy guard. Distrust thyself, and lean more on Jesus. There, only there, wilt thou be safe. Only there, wilt thou be strong. Keep close to Him at all times and in all places, so shall it be well with thy soul.

And if darkness or clouds, films or shadows do come between thee and thy Saviour, haste to the blood! Let not delay beget forgetfulness, and sin secrete itself in the soul. Let nothing harbour or fester in the dark. It is thus that spiritual sensitiveness begins to decline. Tenderness of conscience gives way. Then comes alienation, till, little by little, there is left behind in the soul an earthliness, a deadness, a blank. We have less shrinking from what is contrary to God's Spirit than we once had. Communion with God begins to lose its former freshness and sweetness. Some things, *worldly*, though not perhaps *sinful*, begin to have attractions for us they formerly had not. Then we go on to little compliances, little concessions, which we once could not have made. The line which once separated us from the world becomes less broad and clear and distinct than it used to be. And so we go on, little by little, till we find ourselves at a distance from God and *carried* down the stream of the world. Oh watch, brother, watch! Keep near to Jesus! Haste to the blood! So shall all go well with thy soul.

"Come nearer, nearer still;
  Let not Thy light depart;
Bend, Lord, my selfish will;
  Preserve my wandering heart.

Less wayward let me be,
  More pliable and mild;
In glad simplicity,
  More like a truthful child.

Less, less of self each day,
  And more, my God, of Thee:
Oh keep me in the way,
  However rough it be.

Less of the flesh each hour,
  Less of the world and sin;
More of Thy Spirit's power,
  More of Thyself within.

More moulded to Thy will,
  Lord, let Thy servant be:
Higher and higher still,
  Liker and liker Thee.

Leave nought that is unmeet;
  Of all that is mine own,
Strip me, and so complete
  My training for Thy throne."

CHAPTER VIII.

Assurance and Prayer.

"My Beloved is mine, and I am His : He feedeth among the lilies. Until the day break, and the shadows flee away, turn, my Beloved, and be Thou like a roe or a young hart upon the mountains of Bether." *Song of Sol.* ii. 16, 17.

THE soul never can know true peace till it is able to say, "My Beloved is mine, and I am His." This assurance is the source of praise and thanksgiving, and the spring of devotedness in God's service. If our religion stop short of this, it is worthless. To be able to say, "Jesus is mine, and I am His," imparts to the heart peace, joy, thankfulness, and praise. It lifts it up. It makes it glad and happy. It opens the lips in praise and prayer. It banishes all sadness and gloom. It gives the heart an impetus which nothing else can give. It wakes it up to toil and labour for Christ. It makes all service delightful. To be able to say, "Jesus is mine, and I am His," takes away the sting from death. Without this a dying bed will never be a joyful prospect. It is, it must be, a dark shadow over our way, from which the soul will shrink. The soul that can say, "Jesus is mine," has gotten the victory over death, and is ready whenever the Lord may send for it.

But who may say this? Every poor sinner who comes to Jesus, no matter who or what he may have been. The soul's first look, trembling and hesitating, at Jesus, is everlasting salvation. That soul has all its sins forgiven. That soul *can* say, *should* say, *ought to* say, without one moment's hesitation, "Christ is mine, and I am His." That soul never honours God so much as when in humble confidence it can say this. That soul believes God's word, *really* believes it. When God says in His word, "The blood of Jesus Christ His Son cleanseth from *all* sin," the soul that says, "I believe it; it has cleansed *mine*, sinner though I am," honours God, honours His word, has ceased to make God a liar, and believes on the Lord Jesus Christ.

But is it not presumption? Presumption to believe what God tells us! Is it not the greatest presumption to *doubt* it? If a monarch sent a message of pardon to a condemned criminal, would it be *presumption* for him to believe it? Would not the presumption be to *doubt* it?—to turn round and say to the king, "I *see* your pardon, I *read* it, but *in my heart* I don't believe you"! Would not *this* be presumption? Would not *this* be making him a liar? Could he offer the king a greater insult? And yet how often you offer this insult to God! He has sent you a message, "The Lord hath laid on Him the iniquity of us all;" "I have blotted out as a thick cloud thy transgressions;" "having forgiven you *all* trespasses," and yet you turn round and say, "I *see* it, I *read* it, but in my heart I do not believe it"!

"But I do not see that I am one of the 'all' whose sins were laid on Jesus."

Who are these people then who are thus pardoned? They are sinners. What does the Bible say? "Christ died for the *ungodly.*" Mark, for the *ungodly.* Are not you one of them? Then Christ died for *you.* The Lord hath laid on Him, the iniquities of the *ungodly.* Yours were among them. Why will you not believe what God tells you? Why do you continue to say to God, "I do not believe it"?

"But I am *such* a sinner. You do not know what I have been, or perhaps you would not say these things. My past life, oh I tremble as I look back upon it! Crimes deep and dark, sins black as hell can make them!" Well, what is all this but *ungodliness?* "Christ died for the ungodly." It is simply because you *are* such a sinner that you are the one Jesus died for. It is because you are such a sinner you are so fit for Him. Your sins are great, but His blood is greater. "The blood of Jesus Christ cleanseth from *all* sin,"—from *all* sin, therefore, from *yours.* If you were not *such* a sinner, you would not be the one He died for. Believe what He tells you; only believe.

"But I fear I have no faith; my heart is like stone; my prayers seem to be mockery. I am afraid I have not come to Him as I ought, and that I do not believe as I ought." It is not said He died for those who have a right kind of faith, or who believe as they ought, or who come to Him as they ought. If it did, there would be an end of you. No; He died for the "*ungodly.*" Not for those who have the right kind of faith, but for those who have the *wrong* kind of faith—"the ungodly." Not for those who believe as they ought, or who come as they ought, but for those who do *not* believe as they ought, for those who have *not* come as they ought—for " the *ungodly.*"

"But must I not have faith?" Certainly. Faith is simply to believe what God tells you. "Christ died for the *ungodly.* I am *one* of them; therefore He died for *me.*" This is faith, and it is nothing else than this.

"But am I to believe this *now?* Must I not wait awhile till I am better?" What does God say? "*Now* is the accepted time: now is the day of salvation," —that is to say, "*Now* is the time for you to receive salvation." Wait for nothing, but come, and come *when* God *bids* you—not next year, or next month, or next week, or to-morrow, or the next *hour*, but "*now*," THIS MOMENT. Believe what He tells you, and *you* will have "salvation;" you will have peace and joy. "Only believe." "He that believeth on me *hath* everlasting life."

"I could believe it if I were only *better* than I am; if I could only feel I were more *fit* for it."

You would be satisfied with *yourself* if you were better, would you not? This is just self-righteousness. God's desire is to make you *dissatisfied* with yourself. The *worse* you feel yourself to be, the better. Look upon yourself as vile, hateful, "ungodly." This is the light in which God would have you view yourself. Then, when you view yourself in the *very worst* light, you are what God says you are, "ungodly;" you are just the very one for whom He died, for "Christ died for the *ungodly.*" You want to feel happy *before* you can believe what God tells you. God says you must believe *first*. You must *believe* first, then you will feel happy, not *feel* first before you believe. You will never get peace that way. You must change your plan. Believe *first*, believe *now*, believe because God *tells* you. "Only believe," and peace will be yours.

"This is making salvation a very *easy* thing. Is it, *can* it, be so?" Yes; it is making it a GIFT. Can anything be easier than *to take a gift* from the hand of a friend? What does the Bible say? "The *gift* of God is *eternal life.*" Eternal life—the salvation of the soul—is just a GIFT God is holding out to *ungodly sinners.* Will *you* take it from Him? It is a GREAT gift from a *great* God to great sinners, even to the "*ungodly.*" Will you *take* it? He asks you for no *price*—no prayers, no tears, no right repentance, or right faith. He asks you to take it, to take it *now*, to take it just *as you are*—an "ungodly" one. Will you take it?

"Well, I would take it; I would believe;

but I feel I have not peace." *Peace* comes from just simply believing what God tells you. Believe what He says, and you will have peace. Peace comes from believing, not believing from peace. You cannot help having peace if you take God at His word. Your not having peace, is the evidence that you have never yet believed what God tells you. Believe what He tells you. "Only believe."

"But how shall I *keep* that peace?" As you get peace at first by simply believing what Christ has done for you, so you must *keep* peace by *continuing* to believe what He has done for you. You believed God's word about Christ; believe it still. Your look at Christ as He is revealed in that word, gave you peace; your look at Christ as He is there revealed must *continue* that peace. Believe, and continue to believe. Look to Jesus, and continue to look to Jesus. Then will peace always be yours. Then will you be able to say, "My Beloved is mine, and I am His."

But to proceed with the passage. The food of the believer is Christ, and Christ finds His food among believers. "He feedeth among the lilies," or "among the changed ones." "I am the living bread which came down from heaven, that a man may eat thereof and not die." Here the Lord presents Himself as the food of His people. On the other hand, we have a beautiful instance on record of how He finds *His* food among His people. Behold Him at the well of Sychar, with the dust on His sandals, and the sweat on His brow, after a toilsome walk of nearly forty miles under the scorching beams of an eastern sun! He came to that well, flung Himself jaded and wearied at its mouth, to make known to a poor sin-defiled woman the riches of His grace. He opened her heart to see Himself in all the fulness of His love. He drew her after Him—a vessel filled with His grace; and when His disciples, having returned from buying meat in the city, "prayed Him, saying, Master, eat," He replied, "I have meat to eat that ye know not of; my meat is to do the will of Him that sent me, and to finish His work." Yes, the Lord Jesus had had His meat. He had fed among the changed ones. He had drawn a poor sinful soul after Him, and that was Heaven's meat to Him. It was meat the world knew not of. As we gaze upon this beauteous picture of grace at the well of Sychar, surely we may say, "He feedeth among the lilies."

And now we have the Church's prayer —the prayer of each child of God. "Until the day break, and the shadows flee away, turn, my Beloved, and be Thou like a roe or a young hart on the mountains of Bether." The translation of this passage, as it stands in the original, is much clearer and more beautiful: "Until the day break, and the shadows flee away, *be Thou round about me*, my Beloved." And surely after such a sweet view of the Lord Jesus as has been presented to us in this chapter, we may well take up its closing words as *our* prayer too: "Be Thou, precious Saviour, round about me till that hour arrive when all the dark shadows of this night dispensation shall for ever pass away; till that hour arrive when we shall no longer "see through a glass darkly, but face to face;" when the dim, dark outlines of truth we now see, shall yield to eternity's glorious perfections; when shadows shall no longer cast their outlines on our path, making us shrink and tremble for fear, but when morn's glorious sun shall rise in splendour over our heads, never more to set; when "there shall be no more curse," or crying, or tears, or sorrow, or sin, but when "the throne of God and of the Lamb shall be in it, and "His servants shall serve Him." "Be Thou like a roe or a young hart on the mountains of Bether." Yes, dear Lord, be Thou in our eyes "the glorious and beautiful one," the "morning strong one," till that hour shall arrive! May we see Thee on "the mountains of division"—rising above all the divisions and convulsions of the Church and the world! The convulsions in the Church have thrown up these "mountains of division" and discord and strife and separation. The convulsions of sin and Satan have thrown up " mountains of division" in the world, bringing with them their long, dark catalogue of sorrows and tears, strife and discord, misery, despair, and death. Let us now see Thee coming, in Thy glory and beauty and strength, having all these mountains under Thy feet! Let *us* see Thee, dear Lord, in the midst of the darkness and sin now reigning around us, as the "roe and the young hart on the mountains of Bether."

Till that hour arrive, dear Christian reader, may we see Jesus thus. May our eye and our heart be on " the King in His beauty " and glory and strength ; and may our prayer be," Be Thou, Lord, round about me," my shield, my rock, and high tower of defence, my light in the midst of darkness, my joy in sorrow, my strength in weakness, my life in death, my all in all! May you realize Jesus round about you. May you live near to Him, lean on Him, dwell in His love. May His love be shed abroad in your heart abundantly, drawing you, by its all-powerful influence, to walk in His steps, and to live in all things for His glory. Then will that day break upon you in joy unspeakable and full of glory. Then shall you meet your Saviour and go in with Him to the marriage supper of the Lamb. You shall go no more out. You shall see His face. His name shall be in your forehead. "Everlasting joy shall be upon your head, and sorrow and sighing shall flee away."

" Long did I toil, and knew no earthly rest;
  Far did I rove, and found no certain home;
At last I sought them in His sheltering breast,
  Who opes His arms and bids the weary come:
In Christ I found a home, a rest Divine,
And I since then am His, and He is mine.

Yes, He is mine; and nought of earthly things,
  Not all the charms of pleasure, wealth, or power,
The fame of heroes, or the pomp of kings,
  Could-tempt me to forego His love an hour:
Go, worthless world, I cry, with all that's thine,
Go; I my Saviour's am, and He is mine.

The good I have is from His stores supplied;
  The ill is only what He deems the best:
He for my friend,—I'm rich with nought beside;
  And poor without Him, though of all possessed:

THE CHANGED ONES.

Changes may come,—I take or I resign;
Content while I am His, and He is mine.

Whate'er may change, no change in Him is seen;
   A glorious sun that wanes not nor declines,
Above the clouds and storms He walks unseen,
   And sweetly on His people's darkness shines:
All may depart, I fret not nor repine,
While I my Saviour's am, and He is mine.

While here, alas! I know but half His love,
   But half discern Him, and but half adore;
But when I meet Him in the realms above,
   I hope to love Him better, praise Him more,
And feel and tell amid the choir Divine
How fully I am His, and He is mine."

" It may be in the evening,
   When the work of the day is done,
And you have time to sit in the twilight
   And watch the sinking sun;
While the long bright day dies slowy
   Over the sea,
And the hour grows quiet and holy
   With thoughts of me;
While you hear the village children
   Passing along the street,—
Among those thronging footsteps
   May come the sound of MY FEET:

ASSURANCE AND PRAYER.

Therefore I tell you, Watch!
  By the light of the evening star,
When the room is growing dusky
  As the clouds afar;
Let the door be on the latch
  In your home,
For it may be through the gloaming
  I will come.

"It may be when the midnight
  Is heavy upon the land,
And the black waves lying dumbly
  Along the sand;
When the moonless night draws close,
And the lights are out in the house;
  When the fires burn low and red,
And the watch is ticking loudly
  Beside the bed;
Though you sleep, tired out on your couch,
Still your heart must wake and watch
  In the dark room,
For it may be that at midnight
  I will come.

"It may be at the cock-crow,
When the night is dying slowly
  In the sky,
And the sea looks calm and holy,
Waiting for the dawn of the golden sun
  Which draweth nigh;
When the mists are on the valleys, shading
  The rivers chill,
And my morning star is fading, fading;—
Behold, I say unto you, Watch!
  Over the hill:

Let the door be on the latch
  In your home;
In the chill before the dawning,
Between the night and morning
  I may come.

" It may be in the morning,
When the sun is bright and strong,
And the dew is glittering sharply
  Over the little lawn;
When the waves are laughing loudly
  Along the shore,
And the little birds are singing sweetly
  About the door.
With the long day's work before you,
  You rise up with the sun,
And the neighbours come in to talk a little,
  Of all that must be done;
But remember that I may be the next
  To come in at the door,
To call you from all busy work
  For evermore:
As you work your heart must watch,
For the door is on the latch
  In your room,
And it may be in the morning
  I will come."

So He passèd down my cottage garden,
  By the path that leads to the sea,
Till He came to the turn of the little road,
  Where the birch and laburnum tree

ASSURANCE AND PRAYER.

Lean over and arch the way;
There I saw Him a moment stay,
  And turn once more to me
  As I wept at the cottage door,
And lift up His hands in blessing—
  Then I saw His face no more.
And I stood still in the doorway,
  Leaning against the wall,
Not heeding the fair white roses,
  Though I crushed them, and let them fall,
Only looking down the pathway,
  And looking towards the sea,
And wondering, and wondering
  When He would come back for me,
Till I was aware of an Angel
  Who was going swiftly by,
With the gladness of one who goeth
  In the light of God Most High.
He passed the end of the cottage
  Towards the garden gate,—
(I suppose he was come down
At the setting of the sun,
To comfort some one in the village
  Whose dwelling was desolate,)
And he passed before the door
    Beside my place,
And the likeness of a smile
    Was on his face:—
"Weep not," he said, "for unto you is given,
  To watch for the coming of His feet,
Who is the glory of our blessed heaven;

The work and watching will be very sweet,
   Even in an earthly home,
And in such an hour as ye think not
   He will come."

So I am watching quietly
   Every day:
Whenever the sun shines brightly
   I rise and say,—
Surely it is the shining of His face!
And look unto the gates of His high place,
   Beyond the sea,
For I know He is coming shortly
   To summon me.
And when a shadow falls across the window
   Of my room,
Where I am working my appointed task,
I lift my head to watch the door, and ask
   If He is come;
And the Angel answers sweetly,
   In my home,—
"Only a few more shadows,
   And He will come."

B. M.

Works by the same Author.

PUBLISHED BY

S. W. PARTRIDGE, 9, PATERNOSTER ROW, LONDON.

VOICES FROM THE VALLEY TESTIFYING OF JESUS. Fourth edition, fifth thousand, 3s. 6d.

SPIRITUAL UNFOLDINGS FROM THE WORD OF LIFE. Second edition, 3s. 6d.

GLEANINGS FROM SCRIPTURE. 3s. 6d.

TRUTH IN CHRIST. 3s. 6d.

Sacred Poems and Prose. Seventh edition, 6d.

The Christian Casket; or, Second Series of Sacred Poems and Prose. Seventh thousand, 6d.

Be ye Separate: A word to Christians on sanctioning Amusements. Eighth thousand, 9d. per doz.

Published by S. W. Partridge.

Jesus the Great Attraction. Third edition, 2*d.*

The Threefold Cord—Christ, Victory, Thankfulness. Third edition, 2*d.*

Paul and Agrippa; or, Words of Warning and Counsel. Third edition, 9*d.* per doz.

The Treasure in Earthen Vessels. Fourth edition, 1*d.*

Destruction! What is it? Fourth edition, 9*d.* per doz.

The Two Coverings. Eighth thousand, 6*d.* per doz.

Jesus Only; or, Jesus Said. Fiftieth thousand, Halfpenny.

Jesus' Love. Tenth thousand, six a penny.

Jesus Dit (French). Tenth thousand, six a penny.

How an Ungodly Man may be Saved. Fifth thousand, 1*s.* per 100.

Published by S. W. Partridge.

JUST ISSUED.

Lessons from the Lord's early Ministry. 3d.

A Solemn Warning. 9d. per dozen.

I am Chief of Sinners. 1s. per 100.

REVIEWS.

"Such volumes as these cannot be over-multiplied . . . able, elegant, instructive, and very edifying."—*British Standard.*

"Marked by considerable intellectual power; the doctrine thoroughly sound, and on every occasion clearly stated. The appeals to the heart and conscience are frequent and earnest. Christ is the Alpha and the Omega of all his teaching."—*Record.*

"Deeply spiritual, earnestly practical, and rich in the heart's best sympathies. Model statements of Evangelical truth."—*Our Own Fireside.*

Published by S. W. Partridge.

―――

" Full of fervour, rich in gospel truth, searching and eloquent."—REV. HORATIUS BONAR, D.D.

" Your works are most valuable, and deserve the widest circulation among all sections of the Christian Church."—REV. OCTAVIUS WINSLOW, D.D.

Printed in the USA
CPSIA information can be obtained
at www.ICGtesting.com
LVHW010851061024
793012LV00001B/169